1

THE INVESTOR'S ALMANACK

Rui Zhi Dong © 2024

TABLE OF CONTENTS

4

About

I think a life properly lived is just learn-learn-learn all the time.

I think Berkshire's gained enormously from the investment decisions by learning over time. We're way better off by doing it so long.

The decisions blend and the one feature that comes through is the continuous learning. — Charlie Munger

Munger captures the essence of what it means for me to be a successful speculator, investor, or trader — or following the style of someone like Stanley Druckenmiller, a blend of these — which is the relentless pursuit of knowledge that results in better financial decisions over time.

I've always loved bringing physical books with me to my local cafe first thing in the morning. I'd read for a while, drink some coffee, think and reflect, and then do some writing. These quiet moments of reflection and study have been incredibly valuable to me. They've allowed me to study the greatest financial minds and apply their timeless wisdom to my own investing style. By doing this daily and reflecting on what it means for me, it gives me the opportunity for the lessons to really sink in. The more I can learn this way without having to pay the standard market tuition fee, the more I'd consider that a win.

Whenever I have lost money in the stock market I have always considered that I have learned something; that if I have lost money I have gained experience, so that the money really went for a tuition fee. A man has to have experience and he has to pay for it. — Jesse Livermore

For this book, I've compiled a collection of financial wisdom in the one place. To broaden and gain a diverse range of perspectives, I've included nuggets of wisdom from speculators to fundamentalists.

There are also reflection questions for each day.

You are obviously free to discard them and choose your own as you see fit. Hopefully they will serve to prompt your own questions for self-reflection and insight.

Enjoy!

Day 1

It's not whether you're right or wrong, but how much money you make when you're right and how much you lose when you're wrong.

— *George Soros*

Reflection Questions
- How do I size my trades?
- How do I assess the risk reward ratio of my trades?
- How good am I at cutting losers? How good am I at holding onto multibaggers?

Day 2

The most important change in my trading career occurred when I learned to divorce my ego from the trade.

Trading is a psychological game. Most people think that they're playing against the market, buy the market doesn't care.

You're really playing against yourself.

You have to stop trying to will things to happen in order to prove that you're right.

Listen only to what the market is telling you now. Forget what you thought it was telling you five minutes ago. The sole objective of trading is not to prove you're right, but to hear the cash register ring.

— *Martin S. Schwartz*

Reflection Questions
- When was the last time my ego got involved in a trade? What happened?
- How do I minimize the impact of my ego influencing my decisions?

DAY 3

You're constantly fighting your own emotions.

My first boss had this saying, The higher they go, the cheaper they look.

There's something weird where when a security goes up, every bone in your body wants to buy more of it.

And when it goes down, you're fighting making yourself not sell it. It's just the nature of the beast.

You have to constantly remind yourself why you own that security.

Just because it's going down, doesn't necessarily mean you should sell it. If it's going down, it definitely means you should reevaluate your thesis, but it doesn't mean you should sell it.

And you cannot get crazy when it's going up.

You can talk about not being emotional but it takes incredible discipline to act on that.

— *Stanley Druckenmiller*

Reflection Question
- How do I manage my emotions on big rises as well as big declines?

Day 4

The hope of making the stock market pay your bill is one of the most prolific sources of loss in Wall Street.

There isn't a man in Wall Street who has not lost money trying to make the market pay for an automobile or a bracelet or a motor boat or a painting.

What does a man do when he sets out to make the stock market pay for a sudden need? Why, he merely hopes. He gambles. He therefore runs much greater risks than he would if he were speculating intelligently, in accordance with opinions or beliefs logically arrived at after a dispassionate study of underlying conditions. To begin with, he is after an immediate profit.

He cannot afford to wait.

The market must be nice to him at once if at all.

— *Jesse Livermore*

Reflection Questions

- When was the last time I wanted the market to pay for a sudden need like financial pressure? What happened?
- How do I guard against this in the future?

Day 5

It has taken me years to unlearn everything I was taught, and I probably haven't succeeded yet.

I cite this only because most of what has been written about the markets tells you the way it ought to be, and the successful investors I know do not hold to the way it ought to be, they simply go with what is.

— *Adam Smith*

Listening to uninformed people is worse than having no answers at all.

— *Ray Dalio*

Reflection Questions
- How do I filter new information?
- What can I do to improve my filters so I get less noise and misinformation?

DAY 6

Good judgment is usually the result of experience, and experience frequently the result of bad judgment.

— *Robert Lovett*

Reflection Questions
- What have I learned as a result of past mistakes?
- How do I incorporate those lessons?

DAY 7

Whether I am bullish or bearish, I always try to have both long and short positions — just in case I'm wrong.

— *Jim Rogers*

If you know that you are vulnerable to prediction errors, and if you accept that most "risk measures" are flawed because of the Black Swan, then your strategy is to be as hyperconservative and hyperaggressive as you can be instead of being mildly aggressive or conservative.

— *Nassim Taleb*

Reflection Question
- How do I prepare my portfolio for large unexpected market events?

DAY 8

I didn't lose that kind of money simply because of a faulty analysis.

It was the psychological distortion accompanying a series of successes, drawing my ego into the market position and setting me up for the disastrous loss.

All too often a meteoric rise triggers a precipitous fall. Personalizing success sets people up for disastrous failure.

— *Jim Paul*

Reflection Questions
- When was the last time I personalized my trading success?
- What lessons can I take away from that?

Day 9

I'm always thinking about losing money as opposed to making money. Don't focus on making money; focus on protecting what you have. The most important rule is to play great defense, not great offense.

Everyday I assume every position I have is wrong. I know where my stop risk points are going to be. I do that so I can define my maximum drawdown.

— *Paul Tudor Jones*

The first rule of an investment is don't lose money. And the second rule of an investment is don't forget the first rule.

— *Warren Buffett*

There is a time to make money and a time to not lose money.

— *David Tepper*

I'm more concerned about controlling the downside. Learn to take the losses. The most important thing in making money is not letting your losses get out of hand.

— Martin S. Schwartz

Learn how to take losses quickly and cleanly. Don't expect to be right all the time. If you have a mistake, cut your loss as quickly as possible.

— Bernard Baruch

If a position doesn't feel right as soon as you put it on, don't be embarrassed to change your mind and get right out. If you become unsure about a position, and you don't know what to do, just get out.

— Michael Marcus

The majority of unskilled investors stubbornly hold onto their losses when the losses are small and reasonable. They could get out cheaply, but being emotionally involved and human, they keep waiting and hoping until their loss gets much bigger and costs them dearly.

— William O'Neil

Reflection Questions
- What steps do I take to protect my capital? How often do I assess my risk exposure in my positions?

- How do I manage my emotions to make sure that I'm as emotionally detached as possible?

DAY 10

Michael Marcus taught me one other thing that is absolutely critical. You have to be willing to make mistakes regularly.

There is nothing wrong with it.

Michael taught me about making your best judgment, being wrong, making your next best judgment, being wrong, making your third best judgment, and then doubling your money.

— *Bruce Kovner*

Reflection Questions
- How do I deal with my mistakes?
- Do I accept my mistakes as a part of the investing and trading process?

DAY 11

Decrease your trading volume when you are trading poorly. Increase your volume when you are trading well. Never trade in situations where you don't have control. For example, I don't risk significant amounts of money in front of key reports, since that is gambling, not trading.

— *Paul Tudor Jones*

I believe in streaks. You see it in baseball, you see it in everything else, I see it in investing. Sometimes you're seeing the ball, sometimes you're not.

You can be far more aggressive when you're making good profits.

One of my number one jobs is to know when I'm hot or cold. When I'm hot, I'm suppose to turn the dial way up. Not say okay I'm up 40% this year, this will look good end of year, let's go take a break.

No you've got to make hay when you're hot.

And then when you're cold, the last thing you should do is make big bets to get back to even. You should tone yourself down.

So not only do I have to see the investment that really excites me, I also have to see myself sort of being in a good trading rhythm.

— *Stanley Druckenmiller*

There really is no intelligent reason to increase your trading size if your positions are showing losses.

— *Mark Minervini*

Reflection Questions
- Do I try to make back my losses with bigger positions when I've had a string of trading losses?
- Do I press my advantage during hot streaks when I have them or call it a day too early?

DAY 12

A man must know himself thoroughly if he is going to make a good job out of trading in the speculative markets.

— *Jesse Livermore*

Reflection Questions
- How well do I know my strengths and weaknesses as a trader or investor?
- What can I do to better understand these in myself?

Day 13

The balance between confidence and humility is best learned through extensive experience and mistakes.

A good trader has to have three things: a chronic inability to accept things at face value, to feel continuously unsettled, and to have humility.

— *Michael Steinhardt*

Being a successful trader takes courage.

The courage to try, the courage to fail, the courage to succeed, and the courage to keep on going when the going gets tough.

— *Michael Marcus*

Reflection Question
- When have I lacked conviction when I should have pressed a trade or investment? What happened?

Day 14

First of all, never play macho man with the market.

Second, never overtrade.

— *Paul Tudor Jones*

Someone in the market always knows more than you and will be ready to iron you out.

— *Anonymous*

Reflection Questions
- How do I ensure that I avoid becoming overconfident?
- How will I know when I'm overtrading or getting too confident? What steps can I take to mitigate that?

DAY 15

As long as you stick to your own style, you get the good and bad in your own approach.

Some are good holders of winners, but may hold their losers a little too long.

Others may cut their winners a little short, but are quick to take their losses.

When you try to incorporate someone else's style, you often wind up with the worst of both styles.

I've done that a lot.

— *Michael Marcus*

Reflection Questions
- What's the style that uniquely suits my personality?
- How do I make sure that I stay consistent to my style?

DAY 16

You can't turn a losing streak around by trying harder.

— *Jack Schwager*

Reflection Questions
- How do I mentally deal with losing streaks?
- How do I avoid getting emotional and letting that affect me during painful drawdowns?

DAY 17

Excesses in one direction will lead to an opposite excess in the other direction.

Think of the market baseline as attached to a rubber string.

Any action too far in one direction not only brings you back to the baseline, but leads to an overshoot in the opposite direction.

— *Bob Farrell*

Reflection Questions
- How can I tell when markets reach extreme levels?
- How do I deal with market extremes?

DAY 18

I try not to be too much of a wise guy because during major price moves, they will be right for a portion of it.

What I am really looking for is a consensus that the market is not confirming.

I like to know that there are a lot of people who are going to be wrong.

— *Bruce Kovner*

Reflection Questions
- How do I incorporate market perspectives into my strategy?
- What narratives should I be questioning, including those that I subscribe to?

DAY 19

I'm only rich because I know when I'm wrong.

I basically have survived by recognizing my mistakes.

— *George Soros*

It is not what you don't know that will get you into trouble;
it is what you know for sure that just ain't so.

— *Mark Twain*

Reflection Questions
- When was the last time I made losses thanks to false certainty?
- How can I avoid this pitfall in the future?

DAY 20

The hardest thing in this business is to stay in a bull market from beginning to end, the second hardest thing is to stay out of a bear market from beginning to end.

— *Richard Russell*

Reflection Questions
- What's my strategy for dealing with bull and bear markets?
- How do I make sure that I stay disciplined in my approach?

DAY 21

When everybody is on one side of the boat, you should go to the other side.

Nearly every time I strayed from the herd, I've made a lot of money.

Wandering away from the action is the way to find the new action.

— *Jim Rogers*

In investing, the crowd is wrong much more often than right.

— *Kenneth L. Fisher*

Reflection Questions
- How do I identify what the market consensus is?
- How do I determine whether holding a contrarian position is advantageous?

Day 22

You have to minimize your losses and try to preserve capital for those very few instances where you can make a lot in a very short period of time.

What you can't afford to do is throw away your capital on suboptimal trades.

— *Richard Dennis*

Reflection Questions
- How do I determine whether a trade is worth it? What's my risk-reward cut-off?
- How do I exercise discipline and patience so I only press when there's an optimal trade to me made?

DAY 23

Bear markets have three stages — sharp down, reflexive rebound and a drawn-out fundamental downtrend.

— *Bob Farrell*

Reflection Question
- How do I navigate drawn-out bear markets?

DAY 24

There is nothing so disastrous as a rational investment policy in an irrational world.

— *John Maynard Keynes*

Reflection Question
- How do I trade or invest in markets when marked by extreme irrationality?

DAY 25

Volatility is only good if it's part of a trend and it's giving you entry points within a trend.

We're getting volatility with no trend. When you're going up and down but there's no real trend, that's a nightmare.

You might think that a volatility move is the beginning of a trend and get yourself whipsawed.

— *Stanley Druckenmiller*

Reflection Question
- What do I do to maintain discipline and patience in volatile markets?

DAY 26

There are no new eras — excesses are never permanent.

Whatever the latest hot sector is, it eventually overheats, mean reverts, and then overshoots.

As the fever builds, a chorus of "this time it's different" will be heard, even if those exact words are never used. And of course, it — human nature — is never different.

Markets tend to return to the mean over time.

When stocks go too far in one direction, they come back.

Euphoria and pessimism can cloud people's heads. It's easy to get caught up in the heat of the moment and lose perspective.

— *Bob Farrell*

Reflection Question
- How would you assess where markets currently stand on the spectrum between euphoria and pessimism?

DAY 27

1. Always insist on a margin of safety.
2. This time is never different.
3. Be patient and wait for the fat pitch.
4. Be contrarian.
5. Risk is the permanent loss of capital, never a number.
6. Be leery of leverage.
7. Never invest in something you don't understand.

— *James Montier*

Reflection Question

- Of these seven rules, which one stands out the most to me and why? How can I start applying the rule consistently towards my trading/investing strategy?

DAY 28

The riskiest moment is when you are right.

That's when you're in the most trouble, because you tend to overstay the good decisions.

— *Peter Bernstein*

Reflection Question
- Do I have firm rules for exit? For example, when a better opportunity comes along or when the original thesis has changed.

DAY 29

If you believe we're going to have irresponsible monetary policy and inflation going forward, if it's in a bull phase, you want to own bitcoin, but if it's in a bear phase, you want to own gold.

If we're going to have an inflationary bull market, I want to own bitcoin more than gold and if I thought we're going to have a bear market stagflation type tying, then I want to own more gold.

— *Stanley Druckenmiller*

Reflection Question
- How will my portfolio hold up in various economic environments, including in periods of inflation and stagflation?

DAY 30

Remember that stocks are never too high for you to begin buying or too low to begin selling.

— *Jesse Livermore*

Reflection Questions
- When was the last time I hesitated to sell because the price was too low, or didn't buy because the stock made 52-week highs and I was waiting for a pullback that never came?
- How can I overcome such bias of being price anchored in the future?

Day 31

I can't control what the markets do, but I can control my reactions to what the markets do.

— *Mark Minervini*

The key to trading success is emotional discipline. If intelligence were the key, there would be a lot more people making money trading.

— *Victor Sperandeo*

Reflection Questions
- How do I currently manage my emotional reactions to what markets do?
- What can I do to improve my emotional response?

DAY 32

All past decline look like an opportunity, all future declines look like a risk.

Buy when there's blood in the tweets.

— *Morgan Housel*

Reflection Questions
- How do I prepare myself mentally when there's blood on the street?
- How do I respond to when market sentiment turns overly negative?
- How would I like to respond in such cases?

DAY 33

Investment success doesn't come from "buying good things," but rather from "buying things well."

— *Howard Marks*

Reflection Question
- How do I incorporate margins of safety into my decision making?

DAY 34

The majority of successful traders pick just a few hours of the day to trade and avoid the rest like the plague.

— *Anonymous*

Reflection Question
- How much time do I spend daily looking at my portfolio?
- How can I benefit from restricting my hours of trading?

DAY 35

There is nothing so disturbing to one's well-being and judgment as to see a friend get rich.

— *Charles P. Kindleberger*

If you see lots of people around you who have become fabulously rich by making stupid investments, you begin to think making stupid investments is a good business model.

— *Richard Blum*

Reflection Question
- When was the last time I made a bad investing or trading decision due to FOMO?
- How can I maintain discipline and sidestep foolish trades?

DAY 36

Events of future history will be of the same nature — or nearly so — as the history of the past, so long as men are men.

— *Thucydides*

Reflection Question
- What lessons from past market events should I be studying?

DAY 37

We try not to get into things that we don't understand. And if we're going to lose your money, we want to be able to come before you, you know, next year and tell you we lost your money because we thought this and it turned out to be that.

We don't want to say, you know, somebody wrote us a report saying if, you know, "This is what's going to happen," in some field that we don't understand and that, therefore, we lost your money by following someone else's advice.

So, we won't do it ourselves.

— *Warren Buffett*

Reflection Question
- How do I determine the amount of knowledge I need before investing or trading in a particular asset?

DAY 38

If you are not aggressive, you are not going to make money, and if you are not defensive, you are not going to keep money.

— *Ray Dalio*

Reflection Question
- How do I determine when I need to be aggressive and when to be defensive?

Day 39

The way to make money as a trader is to hate to make money and love to lose money.

The idea is that when you put a trade on and it goes one tick against you, you immediately take your loss.

This happens most of the time but when it goes in your favor, you let it ride and there's an art to this.

Now I do something that's very similar but in a more sophisticated way.

— *Mark Spitznagel*

Reflection Question
- How do I approach losses and winners in my portfolio?

DAY 40

Do not:

1. Sacrifice your position for fluctuations.
2. Expect the market to end in a blaze of glory.
3. Expect the tape to be a lecturer.
4. Try to sell at the top.
5. Imagine that a market that has once sold at 150 must be cheap at 130.
6. Buck the market trend.
7. Look for breaks.
8. Try to make an average from a losing game.
9. Keep goods that show a loss and sell those that show a profit.

— *Amos Hostetter*

Reflection Questions
- Which rule can I benefit the most from?
- How can I implement it in my investing or trading strategy?

DAY 41

1. Price is the most important factor to use in relation to value.

2. Try to establish the value of the company. Remember that a share of stock represents a part of a business and is not just a piece of paper.

3. Use book value as a starting point to try and establish the value of the enterprise. Be sure that debt does not equal 100% of the equity.

4. Have patience. Stocks don't go up immediately.

5. Don't buy on tips or for a quick move. Let the professionals do that, if they can. Don't sell on bad news.

6. Don't be afraid to be a loner but be sure that you are correct in your judgment. You can't be 100% certain but try to look for the weaknesses in your thinking. Buy on a scale down and sell on a scale up.

7. Have the courage of your convictions once you have made a decision.

8. Have a philosophy of investment and try to follow it. The above is a way that I've found successful.

— *Walter Schloss*

Reflection Questions
- Which rule can I benefit the most from?

- How can I incorporate it into my investing or trading strategy?

Day 42

No one ever gets hit by the trade they see coming.

— *Jeff Currie*

Reflection Question
- How do I prepare for risks that are not obvious?
- How do I avoid getting wiped out?
- What am I missing?

DAY 43

In baseball, you can hit 40 home runs on a single-A-league team and never get paid a thing. But in a hedge fund, you get paid on your batting average. So you go to the worst league you can find, where there's the least competition.

— *Julian Robertson*

Reflection Questions
- Am I competing in the A-leagues or do I focus on less competitive areas where I have a bigger edge?
- Is there a better hunting ground for me to explore?

DAY 44

Everyone tends to see the same things, read the same newspapers and get the same data feeds.

The only way to arrive at a different answer from everybody else is to organize the data in different ways, or bring to the analytic process things that are not typically present.

— *Bill Miller*

When most people come to believe the same thing, large gaps open up between price and value.

— *Michael J. Mauboussin*

The only way one makes money in the market is when the market's perception of a stock changes.

— *Robert Wilson*

Reflection Questions
- What do I do differently to others that helps me come up with unique insights?

DAY 45

Win or lose, everybody gets what they want out of the market.

Some people seem to like to lose, so they win by losing money.

— *Ed Seykota*

Reflection Questions
- What is it that I really want from the market?
- Has my behavior reflected that?

DAY 46

When a trader starts to feel really smart, he/she is headed for a huge drawdown.

— *Peter Brandt*

We have nothing to fear but the lack of fear itself.

— *Walter Deemer*

Reflection Question
- What are the warning signs I need to lookout for that I'm becoming overconfident?

DAY 47

Inflationary recessions create monetary illusions.

— *Paulo Macro*

Reflection Question
- How might an inflationary recession distort the financial metrics and economic indicators that I'm looking at?

Day 48

I want market makers, people who know that anything can happen.

The type of guy I don't want is an analyst who has never traded— the type of person who does a calculation on a computer, figures out where a market should be, puts on a big trade, gets caught up in it, and doesn't stop out. And the market is always wrong; he's not. Market makers know that the market is always right. Market makers have that drilled into their head.

I look for the type of guy in London who gets up at seven am on Sunday when his kids are still in bed, logs onto a poker site so that he can pick off the US drunks coming home on Saturday night. He usually clears 5 or 10 grand every Sunday morning before breakfast taking out the drunks playing poker. That's the type of guy you want. Someone who understands an edge.

Analysts, on the other hand, don't think about anything else other than how smart they are.

— *Michael Platt*

Reflection Questions

- What qualities and characteristics do I value most in myself?
- What qualities and characteristics do I want to improve the most in myself?

DAY 49

Unlike art, shares need to be purchased with mercenary intent.

A good company doesn't necessarily make a good investment.

It's all about the price you pay.

— *Kerr Neilson*

Reflection Questions
- Do I view my investments and trades with emotional detachment?
- If not, what are some steps I can take to improve the way I view them?

DAY 50

Risk mitigation has both a defensive and offensive component.

Buying when blood is running on the streets is the ultimate value investing approach.

Tail hedging is a cousin to value investing because value investors understand that risk mitigation should really be a source of benefit. It should not just be a source of lowering risk or hiding away in the dark when dark clouds approach. The cure should not be worse than the disease.

Risk mitigation should be something where you are actually wealthier later. This is antithetical to the teachings of modern finance.

— *Mark Spitznagel*

The essence of investment management is the management of risk and not the management of returns.

— *Benjamin Graham*

Reflection Questions

- How do I incorporate risk management into my investing or trading strategy?

Day 51

You can do all the research, all the preparation, whatever.

Your best trade is still going to be you being calm and thinking more clearly when everyone is at an emotional extreme.

Happens maybe once a year if you're lucky.

— *Citrini*

Reflection Question
- What can I do to maintain composure during turbulent times?

DAY 52

My partner Charlie says there are only three ways a smart person can go broke: liquor, ladies, and leverage.

Now the truth is, the first two he just added because they started with L.

It's leverage.

— *Warren Buffett*

Reflection Question
- How do I manage the risks associated with leverage (if used)?

DAY 53

Forget about investors that are missing the forest for the trees.

Today they're so focused on the bark that they don't even see the trees.

— *Seth Klarman*

Reflection Questions
- How do I make sure that I don't lose sight of the bigger picture?

DAY 54

Information, like food, has a sell by date, after all, next quarter's earnings are worthless after next quarter.

And it is for this reason that the information that Zak and I weigh most heavily in thinking about a firm is that which has the longest shelf life, with the highest weighting going to information that is almost axiomatic: it is, in our opinion, the most valuable information.

No doubt Charles Darwin would agree.

— *Nick Sleep*

Reflection Question
- How do I identify what information to focus on and what to ignore? What would I improve about this?

DAY 55

My approach works not by making valid predictions but by allowing me to correct false ones.

My financial success stands in stark contrast with my ability to forecast events.

The outstanding feature of my predictions is that I keep on expecting developments that do not materialize.

All my forecasts are extremely tentative and subject to constant revision in the light of market developments.

The best that can be said is that my framework enables me to understand the significance of events as they unfold.

— *George Soros*

Reflection Question
- How flexible am I in adjusting my beliefs and thesis when contrary facts develop?

DAY 56

Understand who you are as an investor, because you will be tested.

You will have to ask yourself if you truly are a value investor.

— *Li Lu*

If you are going to be a great investor, you have to fit the style to who you are.

At one point I recognized that Warren Buffett, though he had every advantage in learning from Ben Graham, did not copy Ben Graham, but rather set out on his own path, and ran money his way, by his own rules.

I also immediately internalized the idea that no school could teach someone how to be a great investor. If it were true, it'd be the most popular school in the world, with an impossibly high tuition. So it must not be true.

— *Michael Burry*

Reflection Question

- How do I define my investing style, and which investor or combination of investors does it resemble most?

DAY 57

There's always something to worry about.

Everyone has got the brain power to be in the stock market, the question is whether they have the stomach.

People thought the only reason we got out of the 1930's depression was WWII. And they figured the next time we have a recession, we will have another depression — and it's going to be a Great Depression.

So people weren't buying stocks in the 50's cause they thought another depression would happen. In addition, they were very scared about nuclear war. Something about going to Vermont, building a fall-out shelter, stocking it with canned goods that doesn't make you want to buy growth stocks.

I think that the older you get, the more nervous you get about all these things. The reason younger people are better investors is that they haven't heard about all these crises.

— *Peter Lynch*

Reflection Question

- How do I let worries affect my investments or trades?
- How do I overcome these?

Day 58

The one thing I've learned about markets over time is that they tend to train you to ignore something and then humiliate you once you figure it doesn't matter.

— *Stanley Druckenmiller*

Reflection Question
- What steps can I take to avoid becoming complacent?

DAY 59

Some people get rich studying artificial intelligence.

Me, I make money studying natural stupidity.

— *Carl Icahn*

Reflection Question
- How do I incorporate my understanding of human psychology into my investing and trading?

DAY 60

We like a reasonable amount of volatility. In our business we want some action.

Tumult is usually good for us.

Generally, those kinds of times when everyone is running around like a chicken with its head cut off that's pretty good for us because they seem to evidence the patterns that we know how to take advantage of.

— *Jim Simons*

Volatility is a symptom that people have no clue of the underlying value.

— *Jeremy Grantham*

Volatility is the price of admission. The prize inside are superior long-term returns. You have to pay the price to get the returns.

— *Morgan Housel*

Reflection Question
- How can I take advantage of volatility?

Day 61

There is a genius on one side of every trade and a dolt on the other, but which is which does not become clear until much later.

— *Leon Lev*

Reflection Question
- Can I argue the other side of the trade as well as the person on the opposite side?

DAY 62

Never fall in love with a stock.

Always have an open mind.

— *Peter Lynch*

Pride is a great banana peel, as are hope, fear and greed.

My biggest slip-ups occurred shortly after I got emotionally involved with positions.

— *Ed Seykota*

Fall in love with people, children and dogs, but not stocks.

— *Barton Biggs*

Reflection Question
- Have I fallen in love with any of my positions?
- Are there any positions where I am too emotionally involved such that I may be overlooking risks?

DAY 63

Those who do not remember the past are condemned to repeat it.

— *George Santayana*

What we learn from history is that people don't learn from history. And you certainly see that in financial markets all the time.

— *Warren Buffett*

One thing all of us have learned is never ignore the lessons of history.

— *Paul Tudor Jones*

Reflection Questions
- What are some of the top lessons I've learned from historical market events?
- What habits can I implement to keep educating myself about past financial history?

DAY 64

No business is attractive at any price.

— *Shelby Davis*

Prices fluctuate more than values. Therein lies opportunity.

— *Joel Greenblatt*

There's good assets and bad assets but good prices and bad prices supercede whether the assets are good or bad.

— *David Abrams*

Reflection Question
- How do I balance the attractiveness of an asset with the price I'm willing to pay for it?

DAY 65

For the most part, we avoided the damage in the short portfolio [during the dot-com bubble] by refusing to sell short anything just because its valuation appeared silly.

We reasoned that twice a silly valuation is not twice as silly. It is still just silly. Kind of like twice of infinity is still infinity.

— *David Einhorn*

While we love catalysts on the long side, we require them on the short side.

— *Shawn Kravetz*

Reflection Questions
- How do I approach overvalued stocks?
- What catalysts am I looking for?
- How do I manage the risk of irrational markets?

DAY 66

A common mistake traders make in shorting is that they take on too big of a position relative to their portfolio. Then when the stock moves against them, the pain becomes too great to handle, and they end up panicking or freezing.

— *Steven Cohen*

Reflection Questions
- How do I manage my positions when they move against me?
- How do I size my positions?

DAY 67

We have two kinds of forecasters, those who don't know and those who don't know they don't know. John Kenneth Galbraith

— *John Kenneth Galbraith*

My financial success stands in stark contrast with my ability to forecast events.

— *George Soros*

Reflection Questions
- How much am I relying on forecasts or predictions for my financial success?

Day 68

Of all the losing investment approaches out there, that of being a pessimistic trader must be the most certain to lead to disappointing returns.

— *Nick Train*

One needs to be an optimist in times of maximum pessimism.

People are always asking me where the outlook is good, but that's the wrong question. The right question is where is the outlook most miserable?

— *Sir John Templeton*

Reflection Questions
- How do I see the current market sentiment on the optimism-pessimism spectrum?

Day 69

The biggest error an investor can make is the sale of a Walmart or a Microsoft in the early stages of the company's growth.

Mathematically, this error is far greater than the equivalent sum invested in a firm that goes bankrupt.

The industry tends to gloss over this fact, perhaps because opportunity costs go unrecorded in performance records.

— *Nick Sleep*

Reflection Questions
- How do I identify the potential for long-term growth?

DAY 70

In an adverse environment when most strategies are not working well, any leverage is too much, and vice versa.

— *Paul Singer*

The lesson of leverage is this: Assume that the worst imaginable outcome will occur and ask whether you can tolerate it.

If the answer is no, then reduce your borrowing.
— *Ed Thorp*

Reflection Questions
- Am I comfortable with the level of leverage (if any) I have at the moment?

DAY 71

Sentimentality about an asset leads to a lack of discipline.

— *Sam Zell*

A common mistake is to think of the market as a personal nemesis. The market, of course, is totally impersonal.

It doesn't care whether you make money or not. Whenever a trader says "I wish" or "I hope" he is engaging in a very destructive way of thinking because it takes attention away from the diagnostic process.

— *Bruce Kovner*

Reflection Questions
- How do I avoid personalizing market movements?

DAY 72

I have a criterion that I can use to identify my mistakes; the behaviour of the market.

— *George Soros*

If you make a mistake, sell as fast as you can.

— *Li Lu*

If you have made a mistake, deal with the mistake, don't compound it.

— *Michael Steinhardt*

Reflection Questions
- How do I typically deal with my mistakes?
- What was the last one that happened and how did I deal with it?
- Are there any current mistakes that I might be ignoring?

DAY 73

Our trading models actually tend to be contrarian, buying stocks recently out of favor and selling those recently in favor.

— *Jim Simons*

Look at the numbers and think for yourself. All the great investors do, and that's what makes them great.

— *David Abrams*

When views are truly contrarian, they are inevitably uncomfortable. Courage and the ability to withstand pain are required.

— *Michael Steinhardt*

Reflection Questions
- How do I typically deal with my mistakes?
- What was the last one that happened and how did I deal with it?
- Are there any current mistakes that I might be ignoring?

DAY 74

Men who can both be right and sit tight are uncommon.

— *Jessie Livermore*

My mantra has always been like that of Milwaukee Braves pitcher Lew Burdette, who once said, "I earn my living from the hungriness of hitters." I earn my living from the hungriness of investors, from their decisiveness, their forcefulness, from their great urge for immediacy.

— *Mark Spitznagel*

If you've done the numbers and are satisfied with them and the principle is right, you just have to grit your teeth and be patient.

— *Peter Cundill*

Reflection Questions
- When was the last time I sold when I should have just done nothing? What happened?
- How can I stay patient and avoid selling too early?

DAY 75

It's often useful in testing a theory to push it to extremes.

— *Warren Buffett*

Once a person has an idea, we then start whacking at it. We invert the concept. Instead of trying to prove a person's idea, we try to kill it, and if we can't kill it then the person is onto something. Whether it is my own idea or someone else's, that is the process we go through.

— *Bruce Berkowitz*

One trick to see the world more clearly is to invert situations. A newspaper headline claiming one third of the population wants something, also tells you two-thirds don't!

— *Nick Sleep*

Reflection Questions
- How can I test my own thesis by pushing them to extremes to help me uncover anything I may have missed?
- How can I incorporate the practice of inverting into my decision-making process?

DAY 76

If you wake up thinking about a position, it's too big.

— *Steve Clarke*

In my younger days I heard someone, I forgot who, remarked 'sell to the sleeping point.' This is a gem of wisdom of the purest ray serene. When we are worried it is because our subconscious mind is trying to telegraph us some message of warning. The wisest course is to sell to the point where one stops worrying.

— *Bernard Baruch*

Reflection Question
- Are there any positions that's keeping me up at night?

Day 77

During periods when we were losing money, I significantly reduced our overall exposure, and raised cash.

— *Michael Steinhardt*

I keep cutting my position size down as I have losing trades. When I am trading poorly, I keep reducing my position size. That way, I will be trading my smallest position when my trading is worst.

— *Paul Tudor Jones*

Reflection Questions
- When do I need to be raising cash?
- Do I have enough dry powder?

DAY 78

Hubris is as much of a threat as Mr Market.

— *Barton Biggs*

Having humility as investors compared to others is our competitive advantage.

— *Francois Rochon*

Reflection Question
- What are the signs that I've gotten too confident?

DAY 79

Never confuse genius with luck and a bull market.

— *John Bogle*

Bull markets make a lot of people very smart.

— *Ed Yardeni*

In this business it's easy to confuse luck with brains.

Luck is largely responsible for my reputation for genius. I don't walk into the office in the morning and say, "Am I smart today?"

I walk in and wonder, "Am I lucky today?"

— *Jim Simons*

Reflection Question
- To what degree has luck played a role in my successes?

DAY 80

The grass is always greener on the side that's fertilized with bullshit.

"Lack of FOMO" has to be one of the most important investing skills.

— *Morgan Housel*

One of the reasons I do not suffer FOMO is because in 21 years of trading I've discovered that almost every player in this game fails to keep the money they've made.

A person's 15 minutes of fame does not excite me.

I assume, usually correctly, they will end with nothing.

— *Tom Dante*

Reflection Questions
- What do I typically do when I experience FOMO?
- How would I prefer to react when I experience FOMO?

DAY 81

We have to practice defensive investing, since many of the outcomes are likely to go against us.

It's more important to ensure survival under negative outcomes than it is to guarantee maximum returns under favorable ones.

— *Howard Marks*

Reflection Question
- How defensive or aggressive should I be at the moment and why?

DAY 82

If a man is both wise and lucky, he will not make the same mistake twice.

But he will make any one of ten thousand brothers or cousins of the original.

— *Jesse Livermore*

Reflection Questions
- What are variations of past mistakes that I find myself repeatedly making?
- What can I do to recognize and avoid such mistakes in the future?

DAY 83

It doesn't matter whether you are a lion or a gazelle, when the sun comes up you better be running.

— *Leon Cooperman*

The main reason why money is lost in stock speculations is not because Wall Street is dishonest, but because so many people persist in thinking that you can make money without working for it and that the stock exchange is the place where this miracle can be performed.

— *Jessie Livermore*

The people that love it like me are so addicted to it and intellectually stimulated by it. If you're not and you're in it only for the money, you have no chance of competing with these people. So every time you buy something, one of them is selling it. If you're with one of the lazy people that are just doing it for the money, you're going to get run over by those people.

— *Stanley Druckenmiller*

Reflection Question

- How hard am I willing to work to stay ahead?

DAY 84

Those who have knowledge don't predict.

Those who predict don't have knowledge.

— *Lao Tzu*

In business, thoughtful whispering works, which makes it all the more remarkable that the investment industry, as well as many economic commentators, spend so much time shouting.

So much commentary espouses certainty on a multitude of issues, and so little of what is said is, at least in our opinion, knowable.

The absolute certainty in the voice of the proponent so often seeks to mask the weakness of the argument. If Zak and I spot this, we metaphorically tune out.

In our opinion, just a few big things in life are knowable. And it is because just a few things are knowable that Nomad has just a few investments.

— *Nick Sleep*

What is surprising is that even the most sophisticated investors, traders and commentators continue to rely on predictions issued by those who have no record of success at such forecasts.

— *Paul Singer*

You cannot predict, but you can prepare.

— *Howard Marks*

Reflection Questions
- How much do I focus on the knowables?
- What are unknowables that I should stop spending time on?

Day 85

There is always a reason for a stock acting the way it does.

But also remember that chances are you will not become acquainted with that reason until sometime in the future, when it is too late to act on it profitably.

— *Jesse Livermore*

The uncertainty is what creates the opportunity. It's the fact that nobody knows what's going on. So our view is things will be fine, it's going to get a little bit worse but you want to take advantage of that when there is great uncertainty. Everyone who is nervous wants out so you can take advantage of that fact.

— *Marc Lasry*

Reflection Question
- What was my approach the last time I invested during extreme uncertainty? How would I handle the situation differently next time?

DAY 86

Roundaboutness is a central idea of Austrian economics though it doesn't get much consideration anymore.

It's the idea that entrepreneurial growth and capitalistic investing is about delayed gratification.

It looks like you're going left in order to later go right so it looks like you're taking a loss now in order to be more productive later. That's what capital investment is all about. It's about higher productivity later.

If you're looking just one step ahead, it looks like you're doing something stupid.

This applies to investing in many ways and to what I do. Patience and delayed gratification is so critical to being a good investor.

— *Mark Spitznagel*

Reflection Questions
- Describe a time when delayed gratification paid off handsomely for me. What happened?

- How can I incorporate more delayed gratification into my thinking

Day 87

The turtles who outrun the hares are learning machines.

— *Charlie Munger*

The power law of compounding cannot only be applied to investing but it can even, and more importantly, be applied to continued learning. Compounding knowledge through a multidisciplinary framework is an individual's greatest enduring advantage.

— *Christopher Begg*

This business requires constant learning, even sometimes abandoning precepts about industries and geographies that no longer apply. If you're not willing or able to do that, I think the environment ahead means you're in for a very tough time.

— *John Burbank*

The secret to being successful from a trading perspective is to have an indefatigable and an undying and unquenchable thirst for information and knowledge.

— *Paul Tudor Jones*

Reflection Question
- What's one habit I can adopt to compound my learning?

Day 88

You almost have to be curious about everything.

Because you never know where you'll get that one major insight.

Your biggest returns will come from no more than ten tremendous insights. That's it.

The only way to build those insights is intense curiosity, intense study.

— *Li Lu*

People who are curious are going to be better investors and better stewards of others' money.

— *Henry Kravis*

Develop into a lifelong self-learner through voracious reading, cultivate curiosity and strive to become a little wiser every day.

— *Charlie Munger*

Reflection Question
- What's one thing I can do daily that will cultivate my sense of curiosity?

Day 89

Just keep accumulating knowledge.

The stuff I learned when I was 20 is useful today. Not in necessarily the same way and not necessarily every day. But it's useful. You're building a database in your mind that is going to pay off over time.

— *Warren Buffett*

Go to places where you can learn. You can learn from every experience, but just provide yourself with the best opportunities to work with people who you think are smart and who you respect.

— *Barry Rosenstein*

Reflection Questions
- Where can I go today to learn something new?
- Who can I reach out to today to learn something?

DAY 90

Life takes funny turns. That's really important.

You've got a long life. Don't get upset by setbacks.

Setbacks are another way to say opportunity.

— *David Tepper*

When I was 47, I was having a difficult year for a variety of reasons and Warren sat me down and said, look, when I was 47 I thought my life was over.

Susie had left me, and I had already accomplished everything I thought was worthwhile as an investor. Berkshire, as far as I knew, was at its peak. And to my surprise, my life kept getting more and more interesting since, and most of the really important things I've done happened after I was 47 and thought my life was over. The reason, he said, was that he had stored up so many experiences, good and bad, in the first part of his life, and as a form of compounding, their positive consequences unreeled over the next thirty-some-odd years.

— *Alice Schroeder on Buffett*